Rain Stained City

Amanda Hawk

BookLeaf Publishing

Presentation by *BookLeaf Publishing*

Web: www.bookleafpub.com

E-mail: info@bookleafpub.com

ISBN: 9789357441490

First edition 2023

*For JD and all my friends with and
without umbrellas.*

The Great Seattle Wheel

At night, we sit back
in a panorama of lights

and drink the stars.
We spin within a neon glow

as Seattle unfolds
into layers of flickers and sparks.

We reach up to find the moon
hiding in the clouds,

and converse with wide eyes, speechless
tongues, and curious fingertips.

We learn to fly in circles
and touch the sky

over and over
with each turn of the wheel.

The Towers of Gas Works Park

The fireworks explode and frame the towers,
and every summer;
it is brought back to 1906-

all spark and fire.
This metal castle lingers over Lake Union
while families gather on the grass mounds

to fly kites, picnic and watch the boats.
It is a skeleton of an old coal gasification plant
converted into a city landmark.

The towers stretch over the lawns,
and people hover in their shadows,
while the pumphouse holds a playground

of picnic tables and children's laughter.
A steampunk backdrop with gated towers and
concrete
among rows of modern homes and electric cars.

Trails and entertainment merge upon this park,
and it becomes one of the best views
to watch the sun set upon the city skyline.

The Stage of Theatre Off Jackson

There is a staircase off Jackson
that leads to a stage beneath the world.
Follow it down with steadfast feet
as you drop into a playground
of burlesque, improv, and literary feasts.
Every seat in the amphitheater
providing the audience with the best view.
Now, sit back and enjoy the sorcery
of the spellbinding performers
as they weave stories from shadows and light
on a stage beneath the world.

Bursts of Color in Monochrome SoDo

SoDo is blotches of gray, black, and dark green
mildew spattered on the buildings.
After six pm, it is a ghost town of daisy tuft
sidewalks,
and glass bottle outlines.

The structures sag beneath the weight of all the
rain
until their paint drips and seeps down the walls
in dark dash lines to guide along hollow
storefront grins.
I make my way along the huddled buildings

to the Showbox collecting music in homaged
hands.
The Starbucks looms and scowls down
at the skeletons clamoring around beneath its
emerald gaze.
I become one inch within its shadow-

a miniature plastic person scooting along a
cardboard backdrop.
I avoid looking up into the envious eyes,
or the graffiti glares of empty display windows.
I find an interruption in the monochrome-

a disruption in the form of bursts of color.
A small gallery for eyes; these four paintings
hang behind glass in swirls of paint,
primary colors and microphones.

An exhibit of Seattle-based singers
explode from the canvas and I stop
to watch their silent symphony
of ache, joy, and love in layers of brush strokes.

Love Poem for Seattle at Night

The city sheds the stern ridges of gray and
muted overcast skies
and comes alive at night.

She dresses up in sequins of neon lights and
stretches
herself along the curve of the Space Needle.

She has an orchestra of open signs.
They illuminate the downtown for her entrance,

and I see her in window silhouettes of raised
glasses,
waltzed shadows and stained glass portraits.

Skyscrapers frame her outline
and she drapes herself over the skyline cranes.

The city is loud with rumbling feet, scraping
hands,
and honking tongues, but she has a lullaby

in rainwater hums and coffee whistle
conversations.
She kisses with bright red flashing marquee lips

and caresses with gritty guitar fingers.
She says I love you in the dew settling on our
cheeks.

Captivity Gallery of Capitol Hill

During the lockdown
I walked across faded
rainbow crosswalks
on to empty sidewalks

in Capitol Hill.
The storefronts
had been boarded up for weeks,
but overnight the wood

came alive with paint brush strokes,
and miles of local artistry.
The Hill became a gallery
for local artists and an escape

for homebound captives.
The blocks bursted into color
with cartoonish grins, ribbons
of inspirational quotes,

and pressed bouquets.
The artwork spreads
from rubber ducky captions in Capitol Hill
to raincoat ducklings in Pioneer Square

to blue and green peacocks near the stadium.
The healing of art radiates throughout the city,
when people needed beauty the most.

Ghosts of Merchant's Cafe and Saloon

The ghosts of Seattle need a break
from their daily grind from time to time.
Since 1890, they have pulled up a stool

at the Merchant's Cafe and Saloon,
and help themselves to the wine and spirits,
the best view of Pioneer Square,

and the scurrying feet of the wait staff.
The staff say if you sit long enough
you can welcome in their whispers,

and can hear them pace back and forth along the
hallways.
They mention you can hear the breaking
of gossamer lace hearts and skip pace giggles of
children.

The staff will tell you about when
they brought in cameras to film
phantom shadows and broken bottles.

The ghosts will remind you they need a break
from themselves from time to time.

They tuck their howls, names and history

in their back pockets or sleeves,
and pull up to watch the living
stumble over curbs, and sway in the streets.

The specters will tell you about gravestones
that fumble to their cars late at night
and head to their manicured graveyards.

Meanwhile, the ghosts of Seattle
pull up a chair at the Merchant's Cafe and
Saloon
and try to remember their home
and wonder if they will ever return one night.

The Beacon of the Seattle Tower

The Seattle Tower looms
over the changing street corners
from dust covered metropolis to modern sheen.

It throws us back into a black and white
projection against the twenty-seven floors
of art deco curves, and floors of arched eyes.

The tower pulses at night
with lamplight and silhouettes,
and is the beacon for all city's ghosts,

while they wander in and out
onto third avenue to the sound
of elevator bells and echoes

of trolley chimes.
All the lost ones find the tower,
and it guards each one
under its stone wings.

Green Lake Sitcom

When I wander around Green Lake,
it reminds me of small town sitcom all serene
with people walking along the path
in pods of family, friends and pets together.
The green of the lawns and trees
stretching up and up above the concrete of the
city.

I forget about the city
when watching the ducks dip up and down in the
lake,
and I get lost within the trees.
I lay upon the lawn and fall into the serene
sky with clouds drifting and merging together
until they form a single homeward path.

The lake is surrounded by a single path
and as I walk it I can see bits and pieces of the
city-
all local taverns, diners bunched together
into graffiti doorways and vacant windows
around the lake.
When I look into the waters rolling serene,
I keep my back to the looming skyscrapers and
face the trees.

I have grown up around trees
and trails into overgrown woods, so I will settle
on an asphalt path
that has me walk around and around in miles of
the serene,
and I can be away from the loud sirens of the
city.
I find a part of myself at Green Lake
and enjoy watching all the families together.

This space is the perfect collection of bird song
and horn blares together.
I spend hours reading books among the trees
or catching a play at the bathhouse theater near
the lake.
Sometimes at night, groups of lanterns float
along the path
and fall into the lake to outshine the city
with each paper shell and candle light flickering
serene.

I want to be a part of the small town serene
and bring all my friends together
at a picnic bench to enjoy this place inside the
city.
I want to gather all the trees
and put them in my pockets, so I can create a
path

from my apartment to Green Lake.

I love the atmosphere of Green Lake with its
fresh air serene-
to follow the path, and gather my thoughts
together.
It is good to have a place of trees in a concrete
city.

Steadfast Home

When Edith told them no,
she introduced them to her mother
in portraits, their years pressed to floorboards,

and the promises to remain folded upon her
couch.
No developers demolished Edith's home,
instead built their concrete fortress around her.

She passed away in 2008,
and her small house stays
nestled between the stone towers

of the Ballard Blocks.
Steadfast, her spirit lingers
behind the chain link fence protection,

where people visit to snap her courage
in photographs, and have her home
tattooed into their skin.

The Ravenna Troll Booth
Never Asked Bettie for a Toll

Bettie Page watched the highway
from her baby blue wall.
Every car zoomed by
with small eye wonder

and steering wheel guidance.
She didn't need
amber horizons anymore.
Bettie settled on the trolls

down the road.
All clay howls and clustered feet,
they sprouted from a fallen maple tree
not far from Ravenna Boulevard.

The trolls split
and multiplied
into a herd of stretched pottery bodies
and handmade twisted grins.

They asked for a toll of a click or an awe
from every passer-by,
except Bettie.
Trolls gathered around her pale legs,

and let the wind howl out every cheer,
until it growled as loud
as the traffic that roared
by Bettie Page's smile.

The Curiosity of the Ave

The shops line both sides of the avenue in
mismatched splendor.
Older buildings built in brick magic and modern
neon.
They hold curiosity in their front windows.
Secondhand trinkets become the focal point of
all the college kids.

Older buildings built with brick magic and
modern neon.
They know how to weave stories with years of
posters plastered to walls.
Secondhand trinkets are the focal point of all the
college kids.
They swarm around entryways in sculptures of
selfies and chatter.

They know how to weave stories within
collegiate years and pamphlets.
The Ave has a ghost of a department store eight
blocks long.
It swarms around entryways of local eateries in
selfies and chatter.
The pride of the area lingers in the street poets,
students, and local shopkeepers.

The Ave is a department store of historical
ghosts.
They hold curiosity in every storefront window.
The pride of the area lingers in the street poets,
students, and local shops.
The magic of the old buildings line both sides of
the avenue in mismatched splendor.

Me and Archie McPhee

The red building brings feet to a stop
so to capture selfies with bigfoot,
crow-headed girl, or a smiling slice of bacon.
The crowd filters through the front door
papered with rubber chickens and punching
nuns,
and find themselves in the wonderland of the
absurd.
Bins of tentacle fingers, retro Barbie happy meal
toys,
and the 80s plastic bell charms provide a time
capsule
back to 1983 when the store began,
while wearable horse heads,
and inflatable unicorn horns for cat bring
everyone back
to modern day weirdness.
Shoppers can explore the worldwide tackiness
in tropical velvet paintings, while going to the
moon
with glow in the dark alien heads.
Archie McPhee is an emporium for the oddballs
and misfits-
the epicenter for the scratch and sniff gag gifts,
mini gadget white elephant presents,

and revamped nativity scenes constructed with
rubber duckies.
It is the perfect escape from traffic jam horns
and time card exits,
and gives people the permission to be free with
each strange contraption.

The Superstar of the Needle

Once the tallest structure
west of the Mississippi,
the Space Needle stretches upward
until the fine point of her tip

Threatens to pop the overcast clouds
into a blue sky.
These days she is in the shadow
of the city skyline, but the people

swarm her base every day.
They climb into her
and she is their rocketship
to catapult them up into the air

so they can touch the face of the sun,
tuck a cloud in their back pocket,
and capture the best selfie,
while the Needle does her spin.

In 1999, the historical society call her
the superstar of the city In flashbulb souvenirs,
and national billboards, and she isn't surprised.
She has been the center of attention since 1962,

and she knows how to give the right angle
for every photo.

Brochure for Pike Place Market

Pike Place Market is a place of flying fish, fresh flowers and herds of feet.
The crowd weaves between booths with serpentine grace.
They gather up all the space needle bobbles, handmade gifts, and a baked treat.

One of the oldest public markets, it stretches along Pike Street.
Every morning, the street vendors line up to find their place.
Pike Place Market isn't just flying fish, fresh flowers and herds of feet.

Established in 1907 for the community to sell produce, fish and meat.
Now, it is home to landscapes, miniature cheesecakes, and fish mouth vases.
The tourists gather up all the space needle bobbles, handmade gifts, and chocolate treats.

Buskers pull out their orchestra of street corner violins, hand pianos for a beat.

People find entertainment in improv, burlesque
and selfie stick spaces.
Pike Place Market is more than a place of flying
fish, fresh flowers and herds of feet.

Folks pose with Rachel and Billie the brass
piggybacks, then enjoy a scenic seat.
Flash snap cameras catch Alaskan Halibut
passes and bright blossom faces.
Folks browse through all the space needle
bobbles, handmade gifts, and powder sugar
treats.

Tourists and locals search for the perfect treasure
to make their trip complete.
The city, local farms, vivid artists, and popular
shops merge in one embrace.
Pike Place Market is a place of flying fish, fresh
flowers and herds of feet.
Everyone gathers up space needle bobbles,
handmade gifts, and a powder sugar treat.

The Best View in Fremont

Ariadne watches the sun set
and the moon rise
from Fremont Peak Park.

She left her silver thread
at the park's entrance
in case anyone got lost.

Every day can be a minotaur
with its stomping problems,
and crashing complications.

She has a home for each one
within a pipe star constellation
hanging in a concrete wall sky.

We all need help in our mazes of thought,
so she brings people here.
To a bluff where people can watch

the sun and moon cycle
the city rush back and forth,
and they can stand still.

Rest Your Hat and Boots in Georgetown

Georgetown is built from brick and brass tacks
And one billboard from the interstate.
It homes steam plants, haunted morgues,
and old west saloons.

In Georgetown's Oxbow Park,
an oversized pair of boots
and cowboy hat finds residence.
Once, they created a gas station

where families stopped and rested,
while filling up their cars
and taking pictures.
They even found themselves

in the backdrop of a major motion picture
about family vacations and chaos,
but these days it nestled in the quiet
between a fence and playground equipment.

Their days tagged in random moments
of children running around them,
teenagers taking selfies, and cars catching
them with gawker's stares.

They wear the sun in rusted wires
and faded paint, and the days
weighed upon their frames.
Hats'n'Boots thought about their main attraction
days

and found their ghosts tucked
beneath chipped colors
then watched as they danced
within the bleached sun's rays.

Under the Marquee of the Paramount Theater

Lights. Camera.
Action and bring on Broadway
beneath the flicker flash marquee

of the Paramount Theater.
A beacon for miles,
crowds flock to enter

stage left or stage right.
We get lost front row seats
for the best musicals, loud music,

and spotlight speakers
and let our minds
fall into every storyline, musical note

and well rehearsed speech.
We all walk beneath the spark flutter marquee
and let the light rest upon our skin

so we can feel like constellation
in the middle of a forest of skyscrapers.

Snapshots of an Afternoon in International District

Wooden dragons twist around the pillars-
all explosions of color and open mouth
amusement.
They are watchers, still-life acrobats
greeting everyone as they walk through
the Historic Chinatown Gate.

Blocks of pinball clangs and bells,
retro games with pink gorilla hands,
and rows of neon manga-
I found myself wandering for hours
one afternoon and getting lost
in the anime robot stares.

I enjoyed green tea, and watched
the family seated around the big table.
They spin the lazy susan in the middle,
while they passed conversation.
My fingers rested upon the chopsticks,
and I decided to call my best friend.

I saw love letters dangle
from the ceiling of Wing Luke Museum,
while bomb sculptures
exploded into flowers in another room.

The night market crowd
clung to me like the summer heat.
I took refuge under the red arch of Hing Hay
Park,
and listened to singing voices cascade
off the wall of bodies.

I listened to someone play violin
in the light rail tunnel and the notes
echoed off the oversize origami cranes.
I admired each metallic fold and bend,
and wrote poems on each crease.

Phantom Dance Halls

I glided into small rooms of red hues
and strobe lights, and made claim to a corner
with stomping feet and swaying arms.
The dance hits of the 80s blurred with electronic
goth

ricocheted off my body, and I felt at home
in misfit crowd of trench coats, spiked hair-
ebbing and flowing from the sidewalks to the
floor,
then spilling back into the streets

in car keys and sweat soaked skin.
Noc Noc, Rebar, and Contour-
My weekend churches
and I worshiped in hips and thighs.

I plucked my younger self from the shadows,
and dressed myself in black.
I found myself on their dance floors
collecting prayers with whiskey hellos and
flirtatious hymns.

These dance hall memories serve as graveyards
when each one closed, and I no longer

do my midnight homages of tired limbs, bar
tabs,
and outcast admiration.

I tried to find a new home in other venues
like the Mercury or Kremwerk,
but my body settled on living rooms and late
night television.
When I go downtown, I see our phantoms

weaving and dancing
outside the board up doorways,
or offering to buy drinks
for the new tenants of the sacred floors.

Kurt in Viretta Park

If you are in Viretta Park at the right moment,
you can see Kurt sitting on the bench
and strumming out his hits

with acoustic fingers and windblown tongue.
He plucks from carved fan names, graffitied
goodbye requests, and pinned lyrical letters,

and recreating a new soundtrack
for outcast ghosts and misfit souls.
The public try to lay him to rest in his hometown

with a giant stone guitar, or sunglass and bone
in a black and white mural near Capitol Hill.
They wedge him behind glass

in a Museum of Pop Culture display, or
give him a memorial near Jimi on Beacon Hill.
Kurt returns to the park, so he can play

his music in bird chirps and traffic rumbles.
His fans make their way
to his benches and press their ears

to listen for his voice.

They know Kurt returns to Viretta Park,
because it isn't far from home.